BE LOVE

Meditative Coloring Book

Adult coloring to open your heart
for relaxation, meditation, stress reduction,
spiritual connection, prayer, centering,
healing, and coming into your deep true
self; ages 9 to 109

Aliyah Schick

Sacred
Imprints

Dedicated to
opening our hearts
to more love
than we can even
imagine,
with it flowing both
outward and inward,
ever more abundantly.

ISBN: 978-0-9882731-5-3

www.MeditativeColoring.com

Books by Aliyah Schick

- Angels Meditative Coloring Book 1
- Crosses Meditative Coloring Book 2
- Ancient Symbols Meditative Coloring Book 3
- Hearts Meditative Coloring Book 4
- Labyrinths Meditative Coloring Book 5
- OM Meditative Coloring Book 6
- Goddess Meditative Coloring Book 7
- Be Love Meditative Coloring Book 8
- Asheville Meditative Coloring Book 9

- Judaica Jewish Coloring Book for Grown Ups
- Chai Jewish Coloring Book for Grown Ups
- Alefbet Jewish Coloring Book for Grown Ups
- Star of David Jewish Coloring Book for Grown Ups

- The Labyrinth Guided Journal, A Year in the Labyrinth
- Mary Magdalene's Words:
    Two Women's Spiritual Journey,
    Both Truth and Fiction, Both Ancient and Now.
- The Mary Magdalene Book: Mary Magdalene Speaks,
    Her Story and Her Message
- Finally, a Book of Poetry by Aliyah Schick

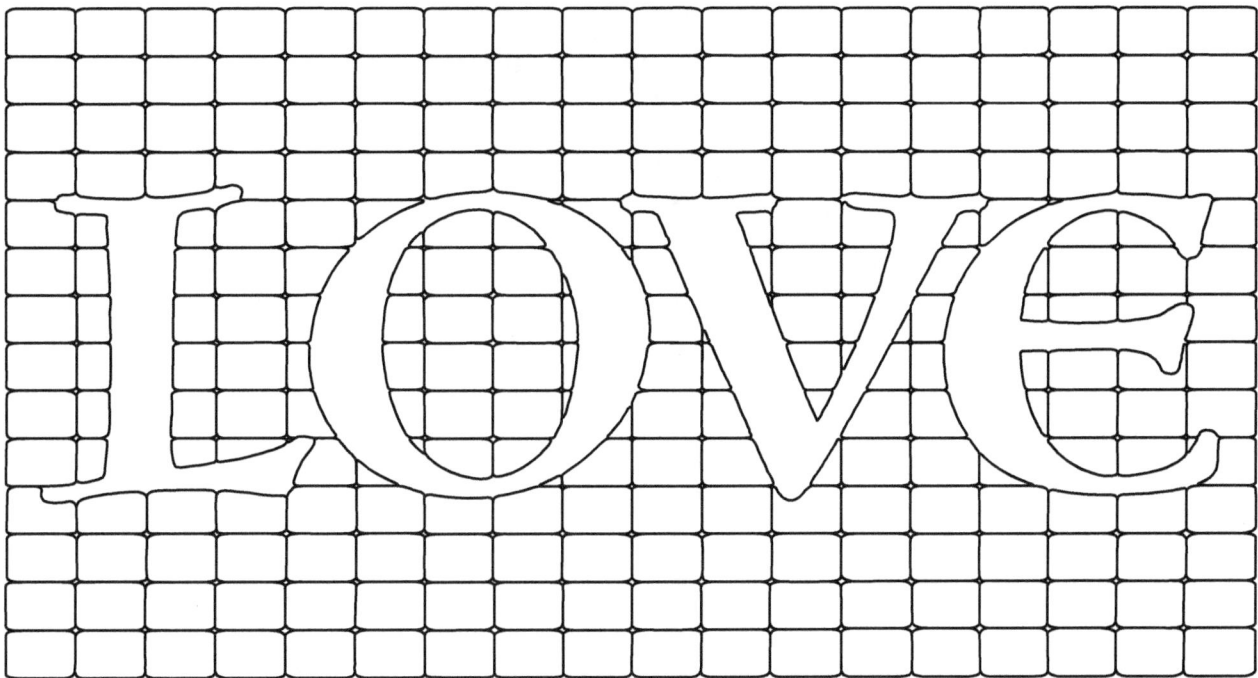

Coloring can be very relaxing and meditative. This book and these drawings are designed to focus your meditative coloring, both consciously and subconsciously, on awakening and expanding the many kinds of love waiting within you.

Love starts inside, with opening yourself to love:

- Color these BE LOVE pages to allow love to blossom all around and through your heart, mind, body, and spirit.
- Color these BE LOVE pages to immerse yourself in the experience and sensations of loving and being loved.

Time spent in love leads to more love,
which leads to more love,
which leads to more love...

All that loving lifts up your life, and Wow!

BE LOVE!

© 2016 Aliyah Schick

Table of Contents

LOVE

There must be a billion ways to love…

- Love life, love self, love family, love mother, love father, love sibling, love child, love grandchild, love great-aunt Sally, love Uncle Frank…

- Love dogs, love cats, love canaries, love cockatiels, love gerbils, love tropical fish, love Clydesdales, love goats…

- Love chickadees, love robins, love raptors, love ducks, love Canadian geese, love puffins, love hummingbirds, love condors…

- Love mountain goats, love tortoises, love wolves, love chipmunks, love deer, love whales, love dolphins, love otters, love jellyfish, love geckos…

- Love sunrise, love sunset, love summer rain, love clouds, love night sky, love sunshine, love seasons, love beach, love sand dunes, love trees, love wildflowers, love mountains, love desert, love rock-strewn streams, love tide pools, love waterfalls, love thunderstorms, love snow, love camping, love fishing, love Yosemite National Park…

- Love creativity, love music, love color, love texture, love architecture, love pattern, love rhythms, love harmony, love art, love language, love writing, love humor, love poetry, love theater, love dance, love song, love chanting, love drum circles, love public speaking, love painting, love coloring, love drawing, love cooking, love decorating, love fashion. Love community, love neighborhood, love country, love friends, love hometown, love culture, love celebrations, love patriotism, love parades, love ethnicity, love diversity, love coming together, love home teams...

- Love baseball, love football, love luge, love bowling, love skiing, love badminton, love soccer, love tennis, love diving, love handball, love Nascar, love competition, love cycling, love playoffs, love winning, love opening day, love playoffs, love the Superbowl, love volleyball, love spinning, love NIA, love yoga, love cross training, love marathons, love Iron Man...

- Love faith, love church/temple/mosque/synagogue, love God/Allah/Great Mother/Jesus/Mary/Universe/Source/The Force, love holy days, love sacred music, love prayer, love meditation, love togetherness, love blessings, love giving, love sharing, love trusting, love believing, love The Circle of Life...

I Love…

I love the opening of the first purple grape hyacinths in the spring.

I love the sound of rain on the roof.

I love seeing the full moon come up through the trees.

I love ducks and geese taking off from the lake.

I love smiling with the checkout clerk at the grocery store.

I love the bounciness of baby goats and kittens.

I love starting a new book, wondering if it will catch me up.

I love listening to owls and woodpeckers.

I love Quizzo night at the beer parlor.

I love live music.

I love misty mountains.

I love ginger ale.

I love out of control giggles.

I love irises.

I love chocolate and caramel.

I love the beach at the edge of the ocean in early morning.

I love a snuggly cat falling asleep in my arms.

I love aerial views of natural land formations.

I love kids playing in mud puddles.

I love waking up to sunshine.

I love clean sheets.

I love homemade coconut oil and peppermint toothpaste.

I love a freedom day with nothing scheduled or expected.

I love completing a game of Sudoku.

I love sending all the trash and recyclables off at the curb.

I love my car easily starting right up.

I love things working out better than even imagined.

I love figuring something out.

I love loving my life.

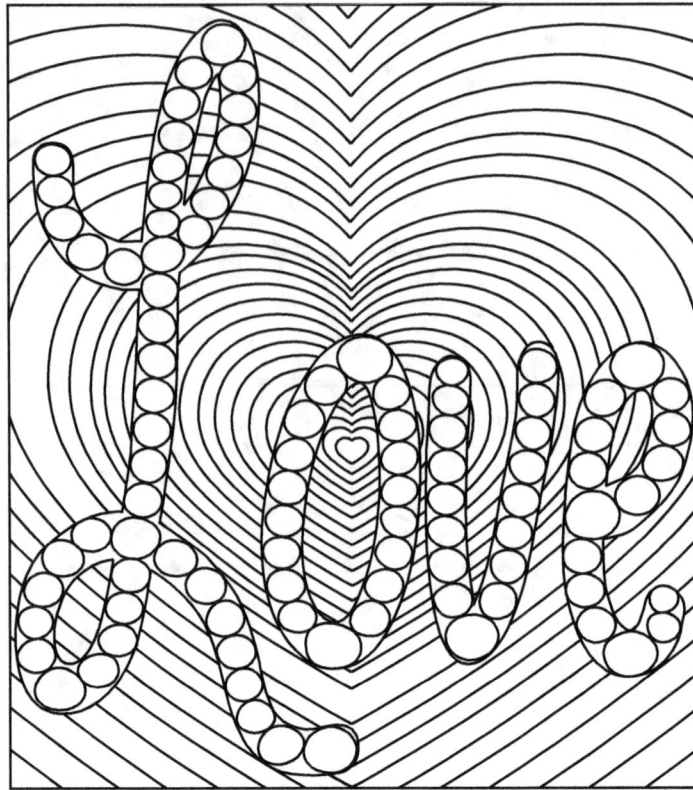

More Things to Love

...cat videos, babies' toes, the Milky Way, baobab trees, mockingbirds, flying, dancing, beer, babies, Olympics, collaboration, downtime, knitting, reading, Rice Krispy Treats, hugs, apple pie, kosher dill pickles, math, astronomy, astrology, paperclips, compost, sex, merry-go-rounds, ferris wheels, bubble gum, fireworks, church bells, grandfather clocks, salt and pepper shakers, diamonds, mani-pedis, flirting, fashion, designer handbags, pink rooms, rock 'n roll, everything country, laughing, late night TV, Dancing with the Stars, Ireland, Sharpie pens, hardware stores, cotton candy, country fairs, politics, investing, nail polish, Twitter, weddings, bouncy castles, road trips, air conditioning, brussels sprouts, Sriracha, flip flops, bare feet, twinkle lights, thick books, romance, blue sky, New Orleans, daydreaming, naps, eggnog, cinnamon, chunky jewelry, fall colors, daffodils, giggles, secrets, velcro, Amazon Prime, apps, freebies, shopping, parties, truth, snuggling, sour balls, soap, fire trucks, fountains, butterflies, polar bears, teddy bears, Barbie dolls, lemon meringue pie...

Add More!

Be Love, Attract Love

We can all use more love in our lives, can't we? More love of life, love for ourselves, love for our work, love for a partner, love for our children, love for our families. And definitely more love coming back at us, too. How can we get more love in our day?

Just about everybody has heard about the Law of Attraction by now. Spiritual teachers have been trying to explain it for eons, and it has now made its way into mainstream culture. Modern physicists starting with Einstein have proved that like attracts like, whether it is a particle or a thought or a rhythm or a person. One vibration or attitude or expectation or focus attracts and encourages others like it. Whatever we put out there attracts more of the same.

The Law of Attraction shows us that it matters what we think about or focus on. If we keep thinking lack and loneliness, that's what we attract. If we want to feel better, we need to choose to focus on what feels better. Having a bad day? Instead of collapsing into a sinkhole of negativity, find something else to fill your mind with happier thoughts. Focus on anything that feels good: a child's birthday, favorite music, the inspiring movie you saw last week, the color you'd like to paint the kitchen, an upcoming vacation...

When you focus on something that feels better, it takes over and lifts your mood. Next thing you know, you're noticing other uplifting things - a song on the radio, a smiling stranger, a great parking space, the sun comes out from behind clouds…

Like attracts like. Feeling good attracts more feel-good happenings.

So, want more love?…

If you want more love you can set yourself up for more love.

There are many recent books and articles about opening to and attracting love. Most of them urge us to first look inward. Be loving in order to attract love. Focus on creating love inside of you, and then love will show up in all sorts of ways all around you.

That's what this BE LOVE Meditative Coloring Book is all about!

Coloring in general is very relaxing, and with a little bit of focus it can be meditative, too. Coloring these BE LOVE pages gets you focused on love while immersing you both consciously and subconsciously into meditating on love. This opens you to all the different kinds of love. It awakens and nourishes the universal experience and sensation of love within you.

Spend time coloring these BE LOVE pages and you spend time in love. Time spent in love attracts more love, which attracts more love, which attracts more love…

The best thing you can do to attract love is to love the love that is already in your life. What do you love? A bite of dark chocolate, Downton Abbey, live comedy, singing to an unborn child, hugs, gardening, coloring, that fresh smell after a rain, lily pads? Love and love some more, and keep loving.

All that loving will attract more and more love from all around you, lift up your life, and wow! Go for it!

Attract Romantic Love

There are many ideas about how to attract that fabulous, passionate, lively, and perfectly balanced relationship. People are making vision boards, using feng shui, meditating on their dream partner, preparing their homes, having makeovers of all kinds from wardrobe to plastic surgery to speech therapy, using dating services, learning about the "Law of Attraction," going to workshops and therapy and spas and gyms and cooking classes and speed dating events and church, and asking friends to fix them up.

There is endless advice in books, in magazines, and online for how to attract true love. And everybody has opinions:

- First, learn to love yourself, learn to value who you really are, learn to treat yourself in loving ways. Only then can you open to being loved by another person.

- Live as if you are already in love with a wonderful person. How would you dress? How would you fix up the house? How would you spend your free time? How would you feel when you wake up each morning? Imagine it's all already true, and live as if it is.

- Be open to receiving love. Practice with someone already in your life by noticing and acknowledging their expression of love for you.

- Do what you really like to do. Enjoy yourself. Have fun.

- Pick a theme song for you and your romantic partner-to-be.

- Watch for reasons to smile. Smile cues are happening all around you. Look for them. Expect them. Smile a lot!

- Spend time with people who are positive and happy about love partnerships. Avoid sharing worries or complaints with those who are frustrated or hurt.

- Take the first step with someone. Just say something or do something—it doesn't have to be perfect or clever or remarkable. It just has to open the moment.

- Help others. Volunteer, reach out, be there, care.

- Stop looking for love. Focus on living your own life in fulfilling ways. Relax about love, and your true love will come to you.

Soulmates

What is a soulmate?

A soulmate relationship is powerful and multifaceted. A soulmate can be a person with whom you feel a profoundly deep, soul-engaging, undeniable connection. You share a compelling love that is unconditional, and you cannot imagine life without them in it. A soulmate can also be your biggest challenge, the one who won't let you get away with anything, who pushes all your buttons, and forces you to live life face on. A soulmate may be your most important influence but possibly not the ideal one to keep close for 24/7.

Do we each have only one perfect soulmate in the whole world?

Most advisors say there are multiple soulmates for each of us. If we are distracted or otherwise unavailable when one comes by, there will be more opportunities for which we can try to be more present.

Are there different kinds of soulmates?

There are many kinds of deep soul connection. Very close friends may be soulmates, as can very close siblings. For some people the relationship with a beloved pet is a soulmate connection. Any profound, soul-based relationship, whether romantic or not, might be considered a soulmate relationship.

How do we find our soulmate?

Our biggest challenge is to get out of our own way. Be ready and available. Be your authentic and honest self, be open and willing, and allow others to see who you are. Be curious and interested in others. You never know where or when or who will show up. Are you ready?

Soulmate Resources

Arielle Ford, *The Soulmate Secret*
Katherine Woodward Thomas, *Calling in "The One"*
Jack Canfield and Mark Victor Hansen, *Chicken Soup for the Soul: True Love*
Daphne Rose Kingma, *The Future of Love*
Marianne Williamson, *Enchanted Love*

Sweethearts

Kermit the Frog and Miss Piggy
Derek Shepard and Meredith Grey
Cleopatra and Antony
Lucille Ball and Desi Arnaz
George Burns and Gracie Allen
Goldie Hawn and Kurt Russell
Lily and Herman Munster
Elvis Presley and Priscilla Presley
Guinevere and Lancelot
Daisy and Donald Duck
Hume Cronyn and Jessica Tandy
Ike and Mamie Eisenhower
Tristan and Isolde
Ethan Hawke and Uma Thurman
Franklin and Eleanor Roosevelt
Napoleon and Josephine
Robin Hood and Maid Marian
Odysseus and Penelope
Edward VIII and Mrs. Simpson
Ronald and Nancy Reagan
Marc Anthony and Jennifer Lopez
Fred and Wilma Flintstone
Henry Higgins and Eliza Doolittle
Scarlett O'Hara and Rhett Butler
Jane Eyre and Rochester
Elizabeth Bennett and Darcy
Tom Cruise and Katie Holmes
Matthew Broderick and Sarah Jessica Parker
Marie and Pierre Curie
Queen Victoria and Prince Albert
Brad Pitt and Angelina Jolie
Abraham Lincoln and Mary Todd
Romeo and Juliet
Akhenaten and Nefertiti
Antonio Banderas and Melanie Griffith
Peter Pan and Wendy Darling

Ross Geller and Rachel Green
Samson and Delilah
Quasimodo and Esmeralda
Bonnie Parker and Clyde Barrow
Courtney Cox and David Arquette
Justin Timberlake and Jessica Biel
Anna and the King of Siam
Lauren Bacall and Humphrey Bogart
Marilyn Monroe and Joe DiMaggio
Maury Povich and Connie Chung
Ozzie and Harriet Nelson
Ma and Pa Kettle
Paul Newman and Joanne Woodward
Prince Charles and Princess Diana
Prince Rainier III and Grace Kelly
Hillary and Bill Clinton
Jennifer Garner and Ben Affleck
Jada Pinkett Smith and Will Smith
Tom Hanks and Rita Wilson
Ward and June Cleaver
John F. and Jackie Kennedy
Phil Donahue and Marlo Thomas
Julius Caesar and Cleopatra
Warren Beatty and Annette Bening
Aladdin and Jasmine
Aragorn and Arwen
Prince William and Kate Middleton
Roy Rogers and Dale Evans
Barbie and Ken
Blondie and Dagwood Bumstead
Cinderella and Prince Charming
Marge and Homer Simpson
Mickey and Minnie Mouse
Rob and Laura Petrie
Rocky Balboa and Adrian
Shrek and Fiona
Tarzan and Jane

Suggestions for How to Use This Book

Use this *Be **Love Meditative Coloring Book*** to spend time immersed in love, in prayer, relaxation, and healing. Come into your deep, true, spiritually attuned, soul self. You may simply wish to experience coloring the images in quiet contemplation. Or, focus on a chant or affirmation as you work with colors. Or, ask for release and understanding regarding an issue you are dealing with. Or, ask for a clearer sense of some aspect of yourself and how it serves you. You may wish to learn more about your path or purpose in this lifetime.

Open your heart and your mind. Pay attention to impressions and ideas, feelings, intuition, and messages. They may very well be exactly what you need to hear.

Tools
Choose your favorite coloring tools, or you might like to gather a variety of pens, crayons, colored pencils, chalk, oil pastels, markers, glitter pens, paints, etc. You may want to place a blank sheet of paper behind the page so ink or paint does not go through.

Music
Consider playing a recording of soft instrumental background music.

Silence
You may prefer quiet, so that all your attention focuses on what you are doing. Emptiness can give rise to profound experience.

Nature
A favorite spot outdoors can provide just the right environment for connecting with your deep self. Beach, woods, backyard, porch, treehouse, mountain top, stream, pond, park, etc.

Meditation
You may like to meditate first, and then begin working with the colors. Try any of the many ways of meditation, or simply be with your breath for a few minutes, following it in and out. Or, you may wish to try the guided meditation on the next page. Read it silently or out loud, slowly, pausing to draw in each breath.

Guided Meditation

Take in a breath... and on the exhale release the day's happenings, settling into this peaceful time of creative, spiritual connection.

Take in a breath... and on the exhale let go of worries and troubles and burdens. You can pick them up again later if you need to.

Take in a breath... and on the exhale come into the center of your self. From there drop a line down through your body, through the chair and the floor and into the earth. Continuing to breathe, drop down through soil and sand and stone, through coal and underground stream, and minerals and precious metals. Down through all the colors and textures and densities of the earth, down to the very center of the earth, to the heart of the mother. Tie your line there. Anchor yourself there.

Take in a breath... and on the exhale extend your line up from your center, through your body and out the crown of your head, up through the ceiling, the roof, and into the sky. Past clouds and wind and thinning gases, out through the atmosphere and into space. Past the sun and galaxy and stars and universe, out to the depths of the Source of All That Is. Feel your connection there. You are part of the great cosmos. You are one with all being.

Take in a breath... and on the exhale return to the drawing before you and ask that you be open to receiving guidance and understanding as you spend time with it. Know that there are no mistakes, only new choices and combinations and patterns that suggest new perception at an other-than-conscious level. Or that remind us of something that can now be released. Or that create an opening to new possibilities.

Take in a breath... and on the exhale release "shoulds" and rules and expectations. Let go and open to new possibilities.

Now, begin by picking up whatever color catches your attention.

About the Artist

Aliyah Schick has been an artist all her life. After Peace Corps in the Andes Mountains of South America, she studied art full time for four years, then created and sold pottery and ceramic art pieces. Later Aliyah worked in fiber and fabric to make soft sculptural wall pieces and art quilts, then fabric dolls designed to carry healing energy. Drawing led to designing her *Meditative Coloring Books*, among the earliest coloring books for grown ups. These continue to be popular because each one is much more than just a coloring book.

At the heart of all this art, Aliyah's deep calling is healing. She is a skilled and dynamic deep energetic healer. Her work in the multidimensional layers and patterns of the auric field is well known, powerful, and effective. Her drawings, paintings, poetry, writings, and *Meditative Coloring Books* emerged as new expressions of Aliyah's healing work. Working with these drawings carries and resonates with that healing, and serves to remind us who we are and why we are here.

Aliyah lives and works in the beautiful Blue Ridge Mountains of North Carolina, where the energy of the earth is easily accessible, ancient, motherly, and obvious. A place where people speak with familiarity and reverence of the land and spirit, and where the sacred comes to sit with us on the porch to share the afternoon sun.

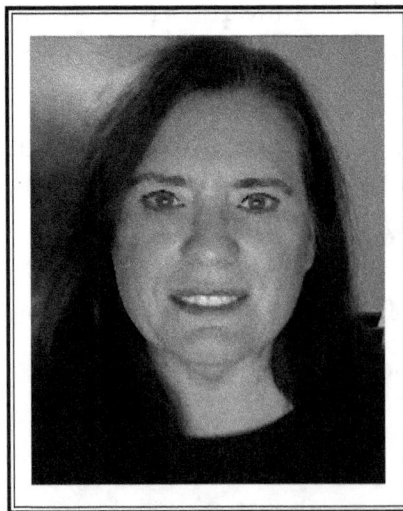

www.AliyahSchick.com

The

Be Love

Drawings

Opposite each Be Love drawing is an inspiring quote and open space labeled Meditative Impressions. Use these pages to catch and keep hold of your thoughts, wishes, intentions, affirmations, prayers, poems, memories, notes, drawings, or whatever comes to you as you explore coloring with this book. Make it yours.

"Let the beauty you love be what you do. There are thousands of ways we kneel and kiss the earth." –Rumi

Meditative Impressions

LOVE

19

"When love isn't in our lives, it's on the way."
–Marianne Williamson

Meditative Impressions

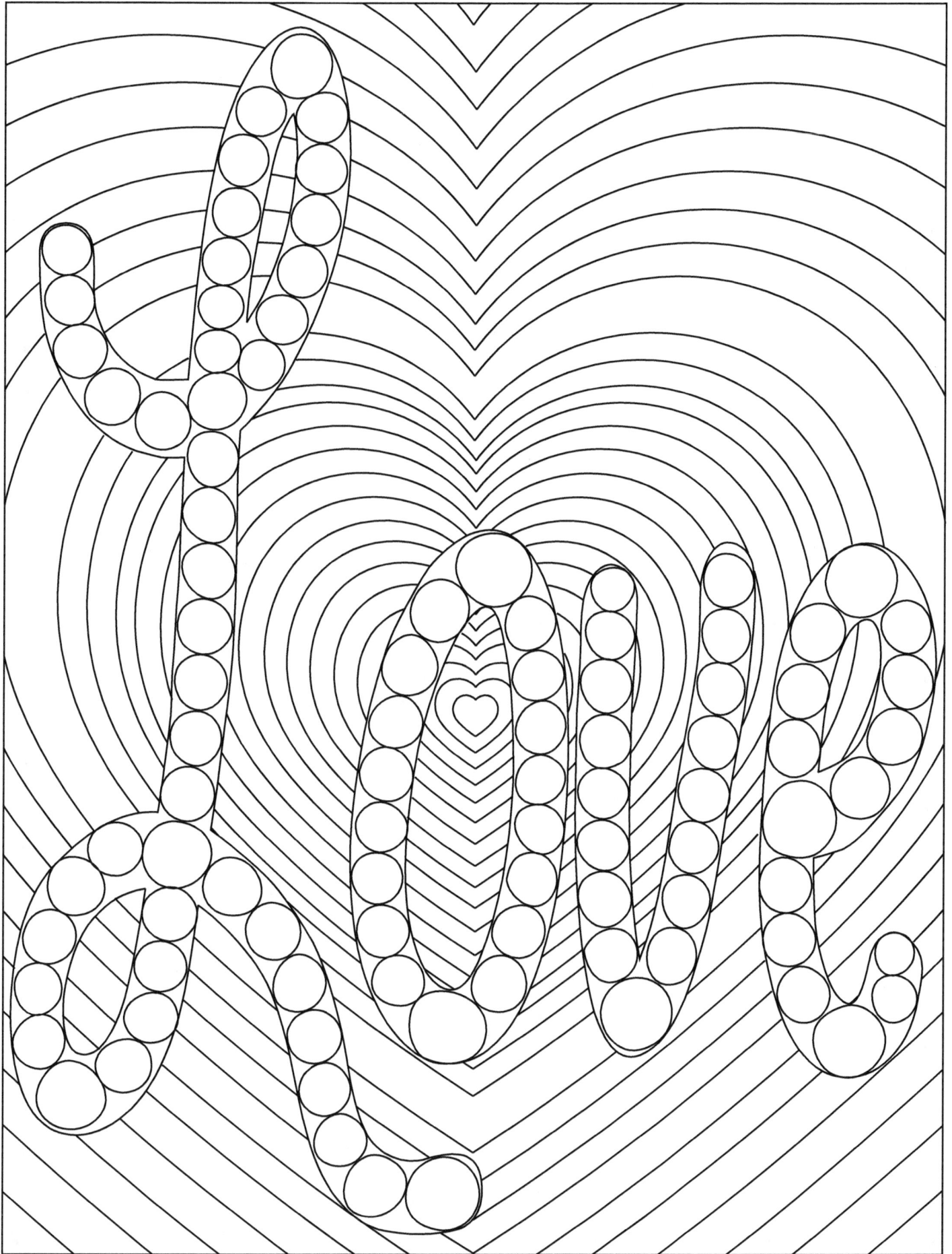

21

"Waking up this morning, I smile. Twenty-four brand new hours are before me. "

-Thich Nhat Hanh

Meditative Impressions

22

23

"If one wishes to know love, one must live love, in action."
-Leo Buscaglia

<u>Meditative Impressions</u>

LOVE
LOVE
LOVE

© 2016 Aliyah Schick

"In our life there is a single color, as on an artist's palatte, which provides the meaning of life and art. It is the color of love."

-Marc Chagall

Meditative Impressions

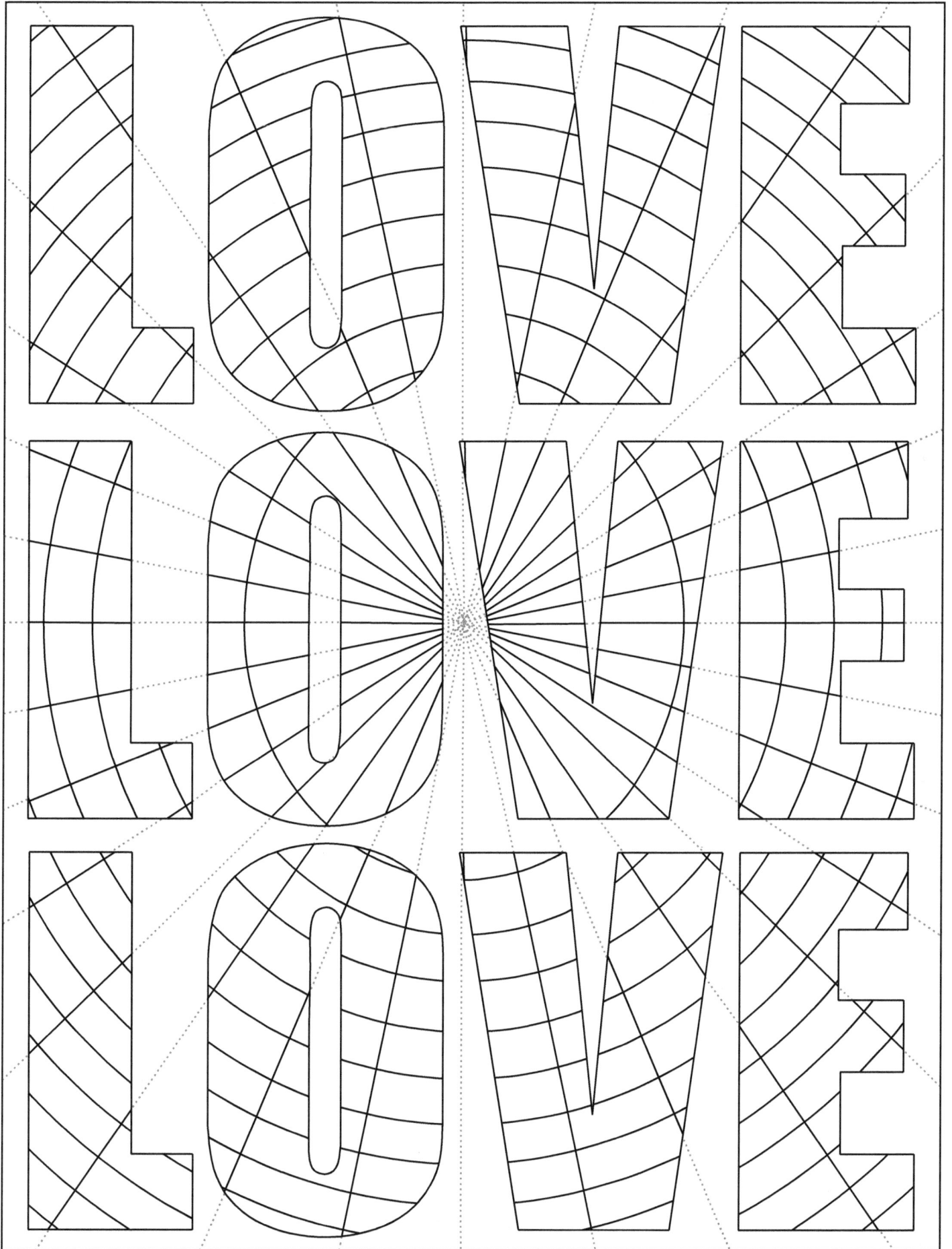

"Love is the flower you've got to let grow."
—John Lennon

Meditative Impressions

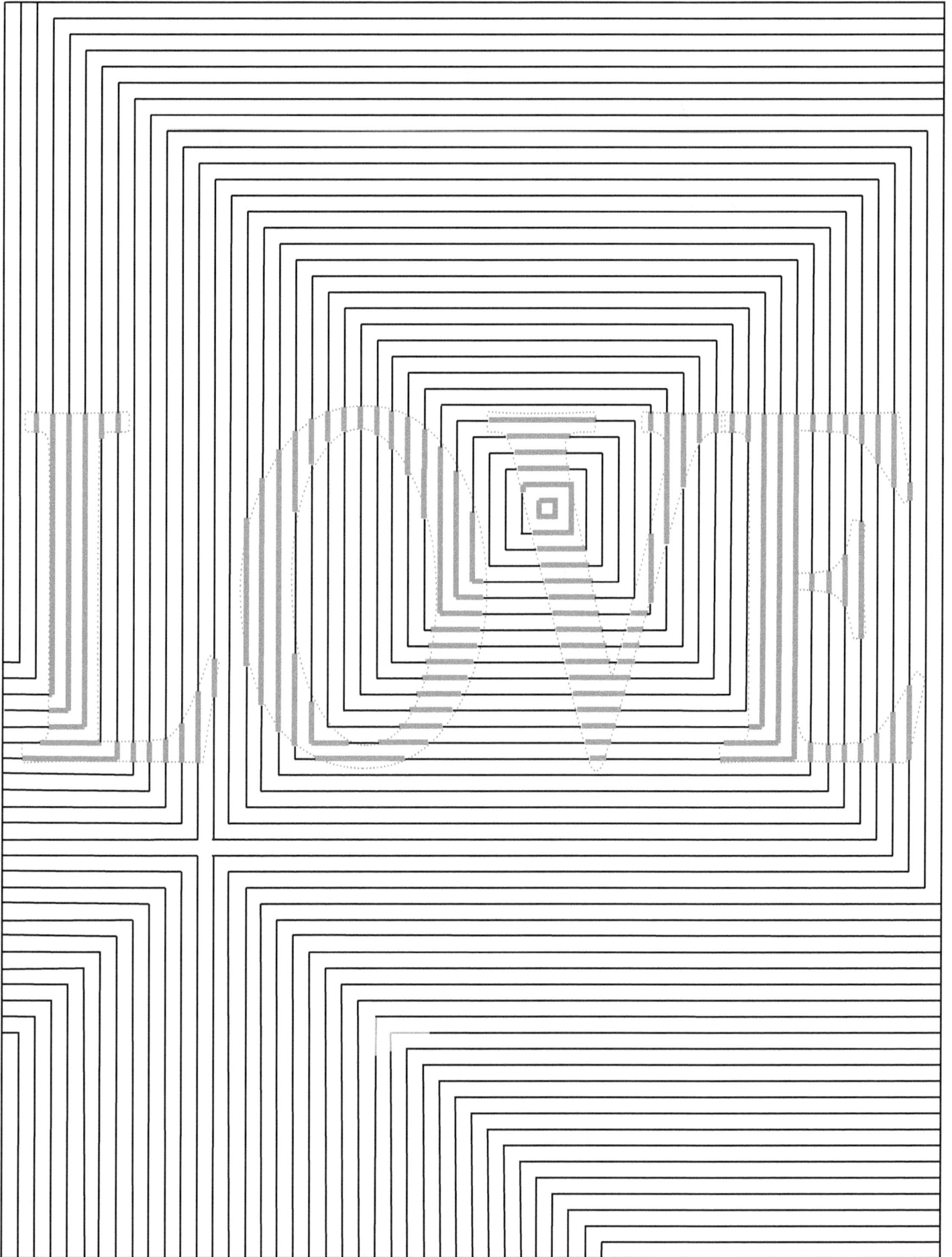

"Love is the most important thing in the world,
but baseball is pretty good, too."

–Greg, age 8

<u>Meditative Impressions</u>

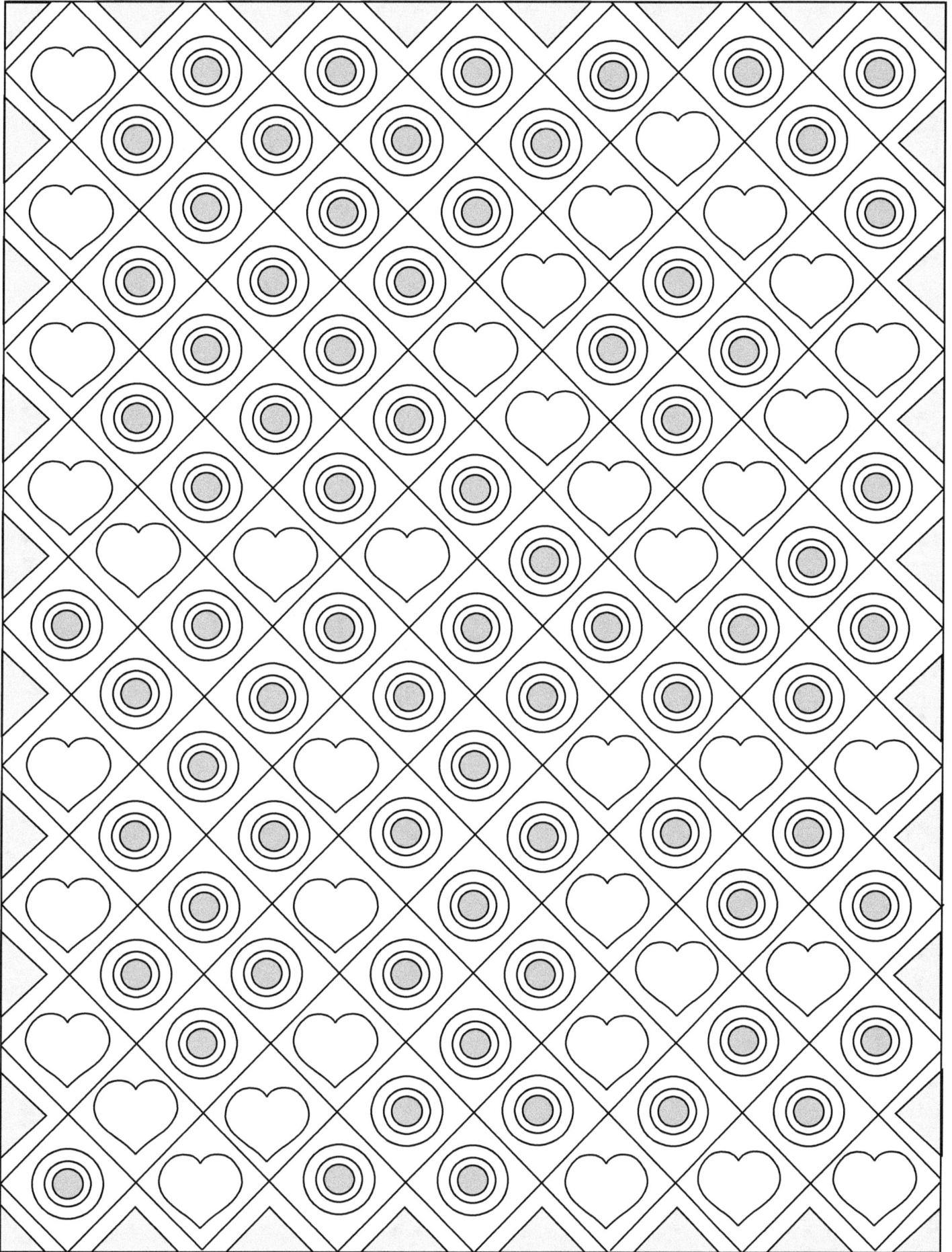

31

"To me every hour of light and dark is a miracle."
                              –Walt Whitman

<u>Meditative Impressions</u>

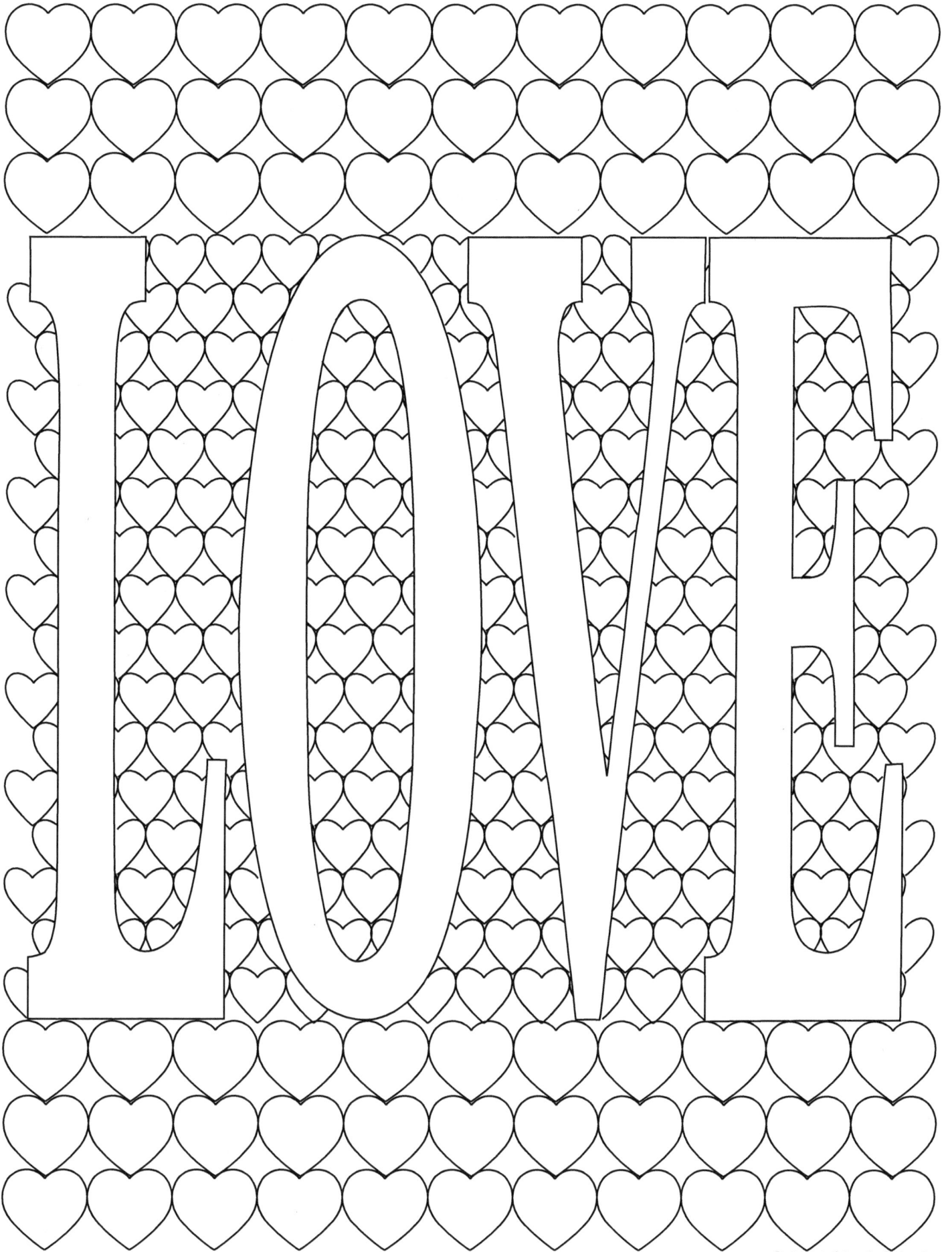

LOVE

33

"It is love, not reason, that is stronger than death."
–Thomas Mann

<u>Meditative Impressions</u>

34

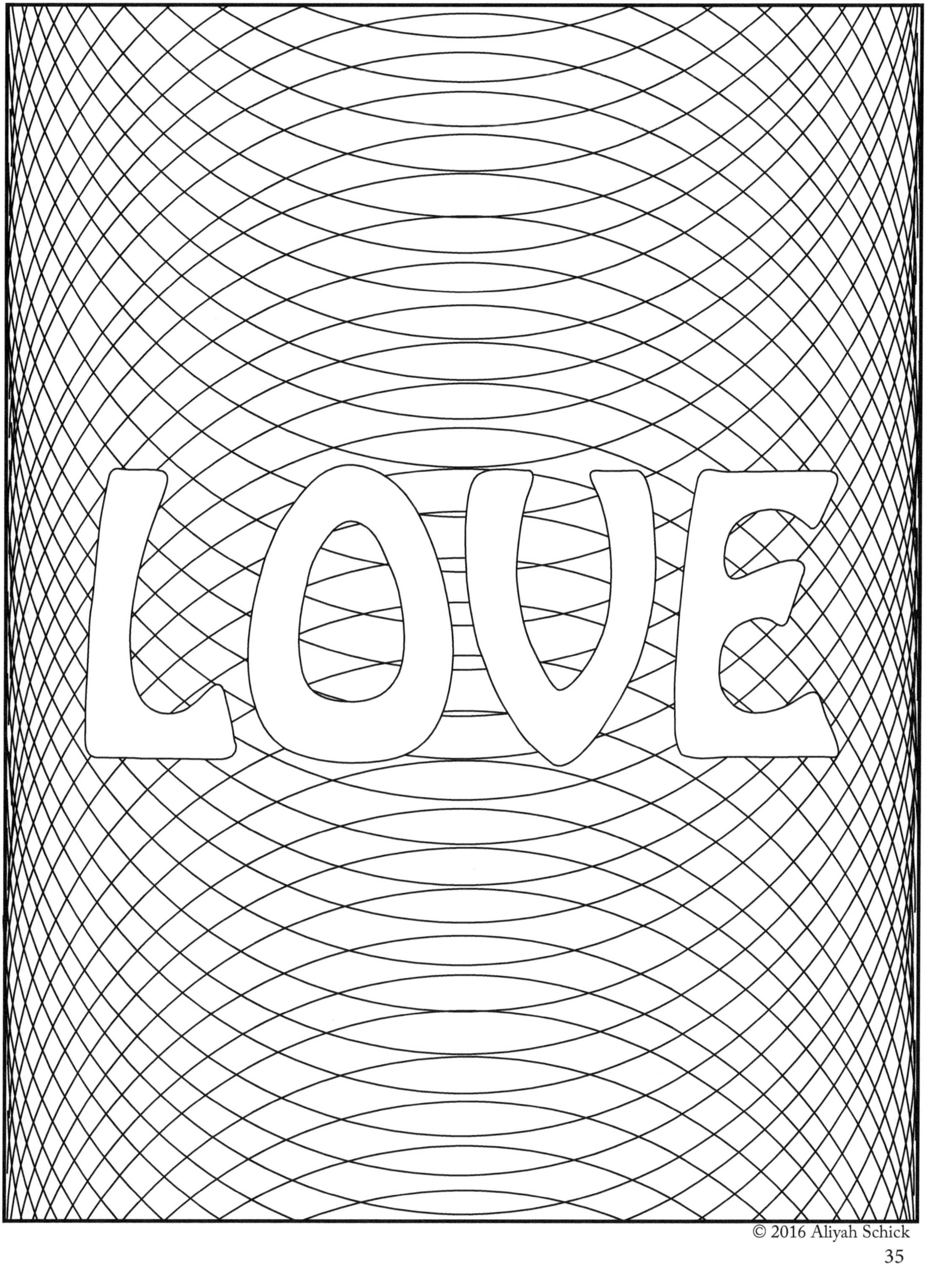
LOVE

"What the world really needs is more love and less paperwork."

-Pearl Bailey

<u>Meditative Impressions</u>

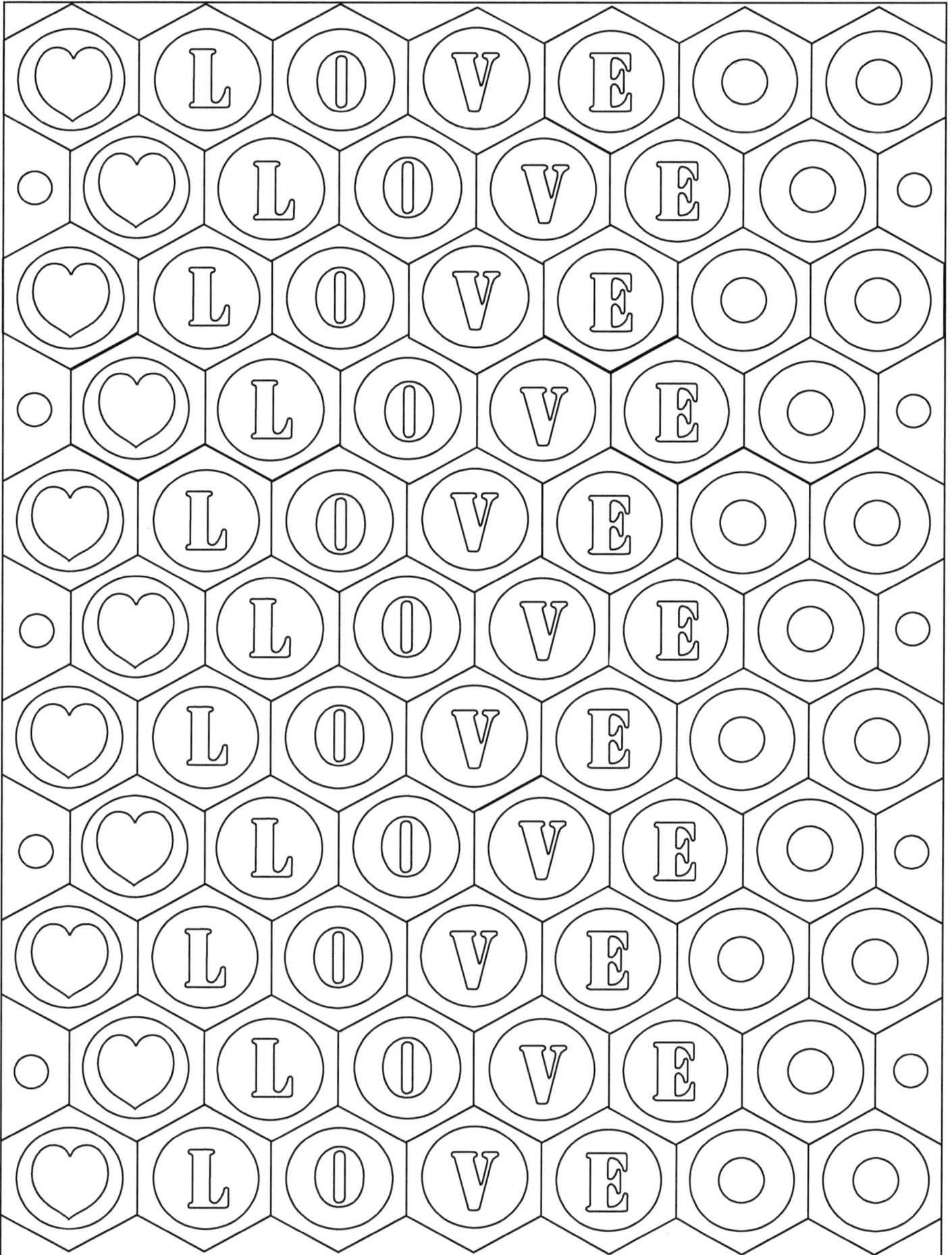

37

"Love is a canvas furnished by Nature and embroidered by imagination."

–Voltaire

<u>Meditative Impressions</u>

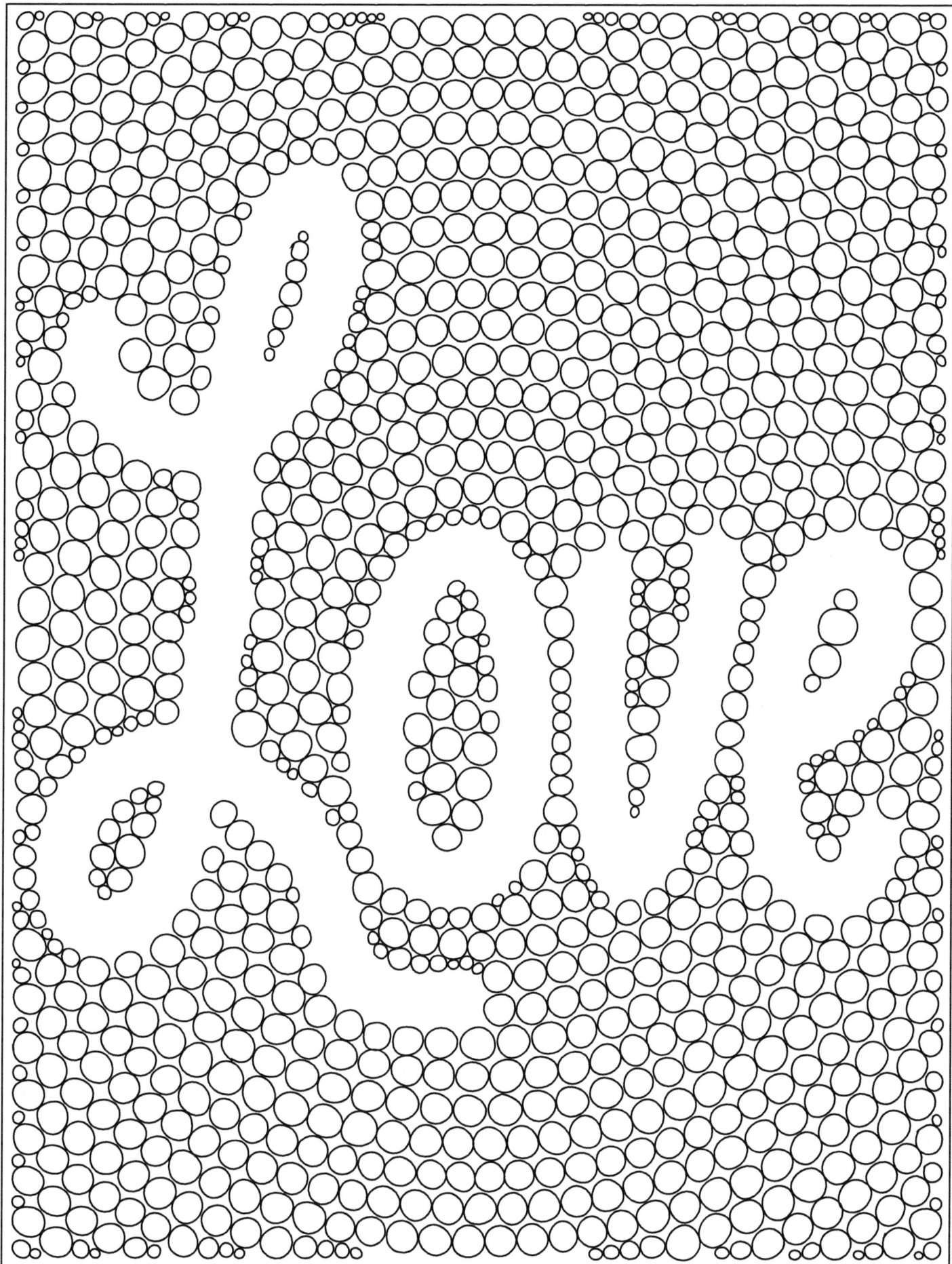

39

"It doesn't matter who you love, or how you love, but that you love."

–Robert Browning
<u>Meditative Impressions</u>

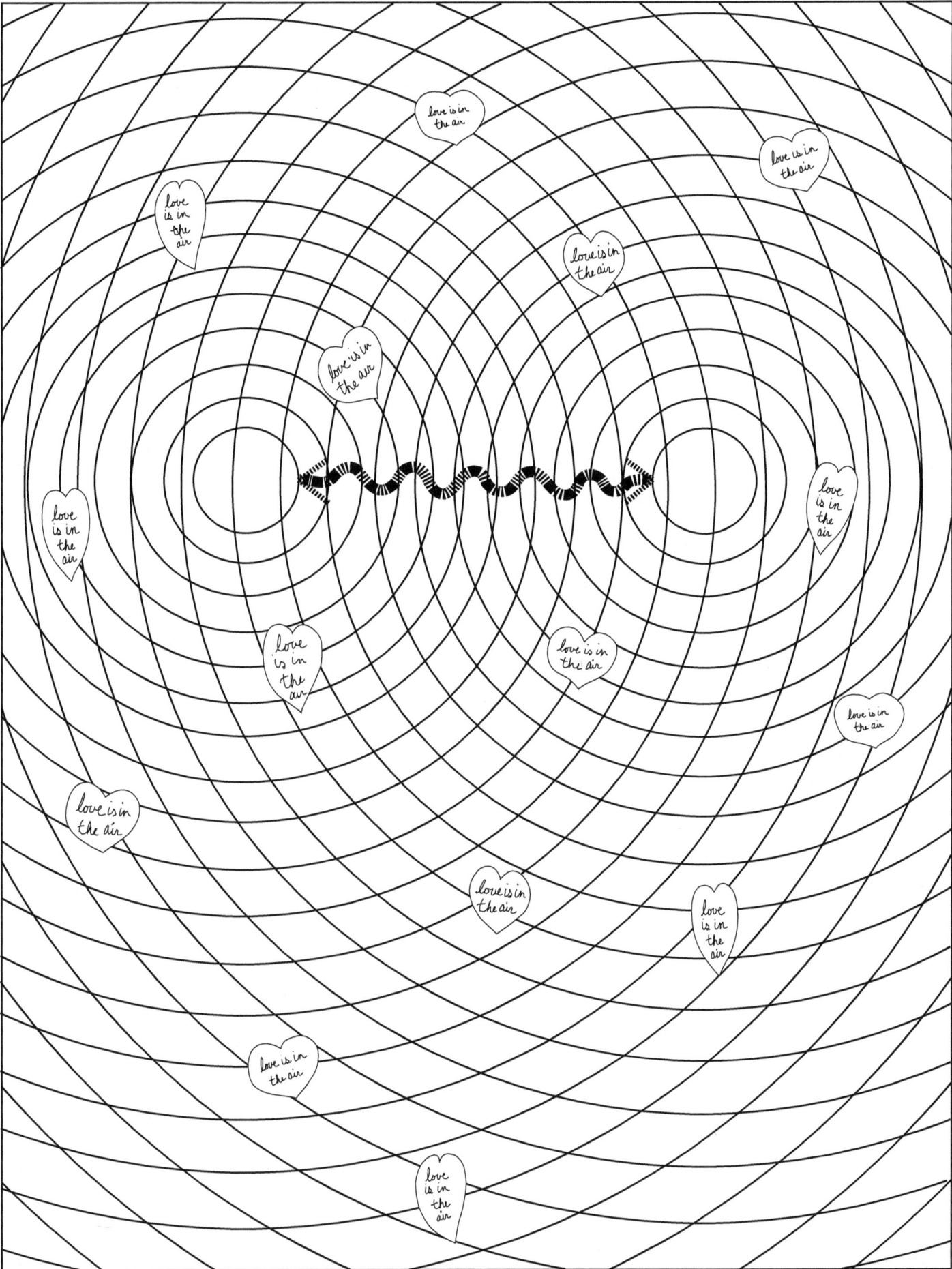

love is in the air

41

"The heart is like a garden. It can grow compassion or fear, resentment or love. What seeds will you plant there?"
                                        –Jack Kornfield

<u>Meditative Impressions</u>

43

"God loves the world through us."
–Mother Teresa

<u>Meditative Impressions</u>

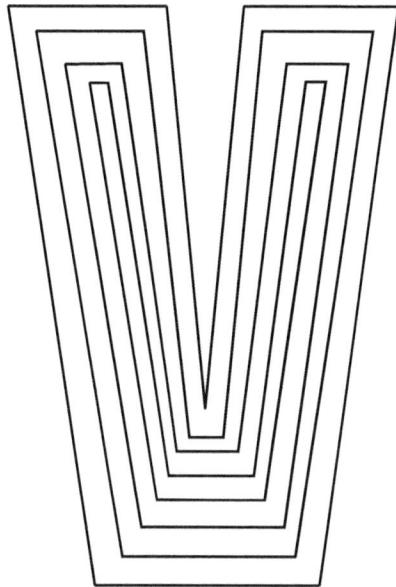

© 2016 Aliyah Schick

*"Love is the only sane and satisfactory answer
to the problems of human existence."*
                                    –Erich Fromm
                        <u>Meditative Impressions</u>

"When we are in love, we open to all that life has to offer, with passion, excitement, and acceptance."
–John Lennon

Meditative Impressions

LOVE

LOVE

LOVE

49

"Your task is not to seek for love, but merely to seek and find all the barriers within yourself that you have built against it."

—Rumi

Meditative Impressions

"One word frees us of all the weight and pain of life.
That word is love."

–Sophocles

Meditative Impressions

53

"Have enough courage to trust love one more time, and always one more time."

–Maya Angelou

<u>Meditative Impressions</u>

"The love we give away is the only love we keep."
-Elbert Hubbard

Meditative Impressions

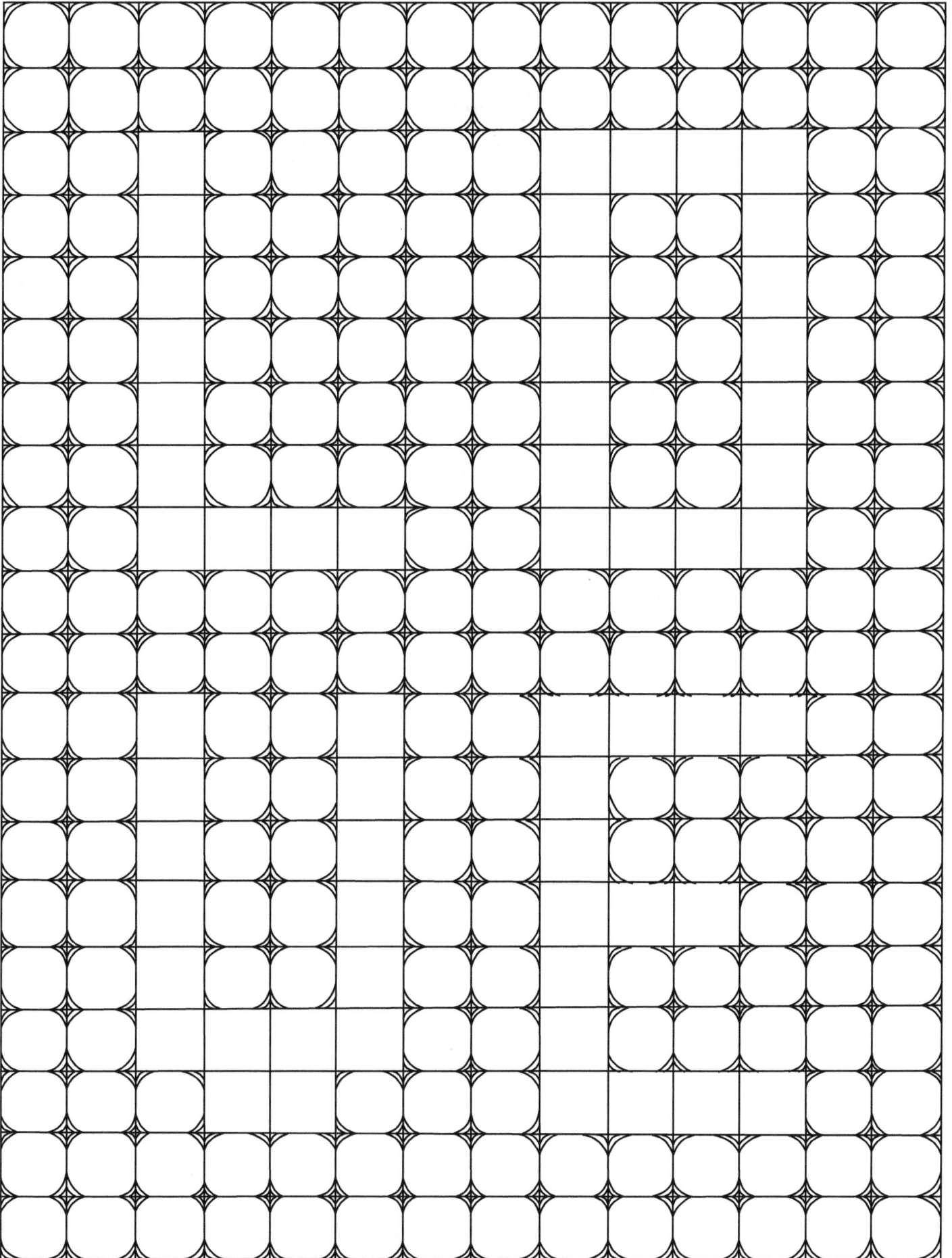

"Love is metaphysical gravity."
                    –R. Buckminster Fuller

<u>Meditative Impressions</u>

"If grass can grow through cement, love can find you at every time of your life."

–Cher

<u>Meditative Impressions</u>

60

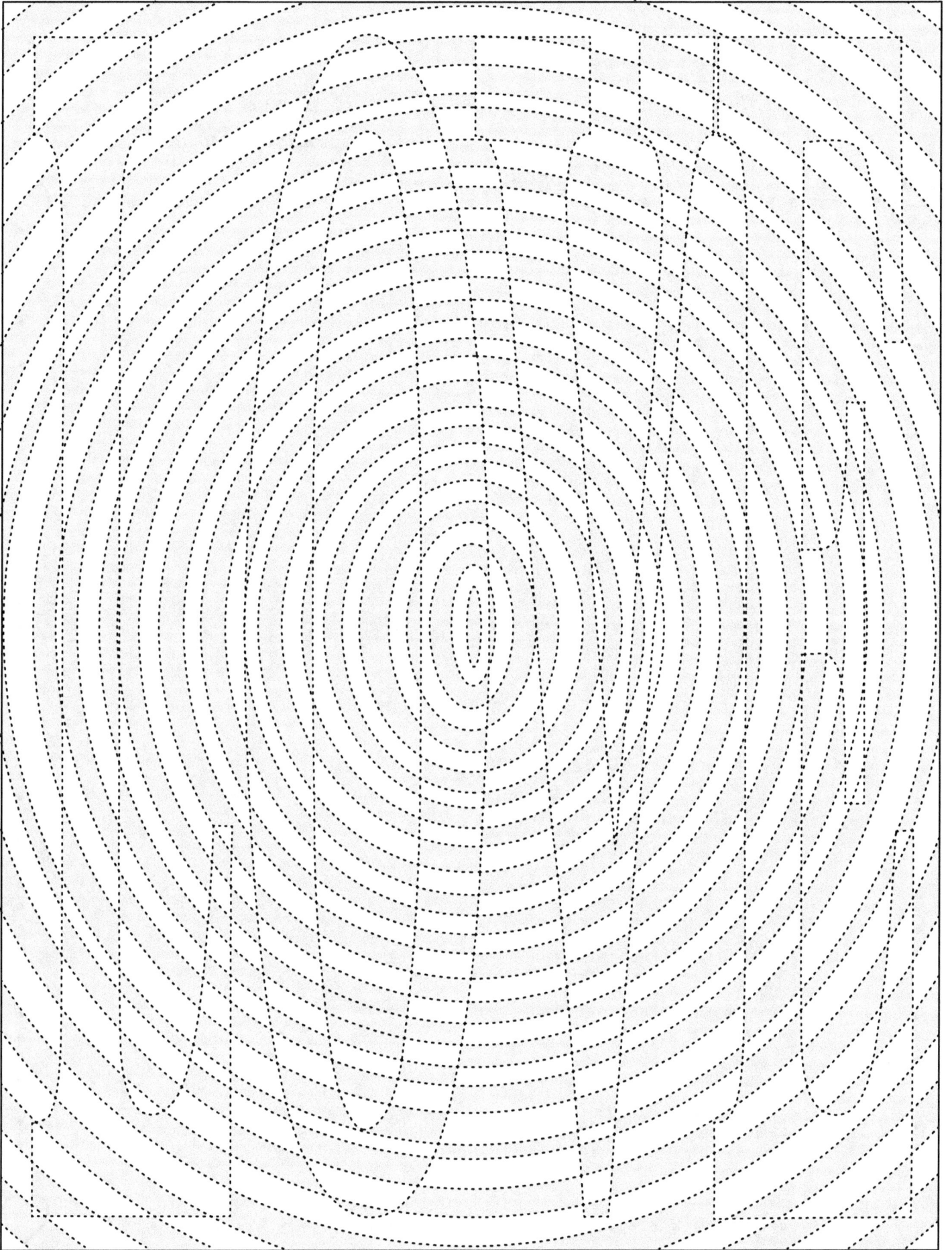

"Life without love is like a tree without blossoms or fruit."
                                        –Khalil Gibran

<u>Meditative Impressions</u>

love

love

love is all around is all around

love love love love

love is all around is all around

love love

63

"People think that love is an emotion. Love is good sense."
                                            –Ken Kesey

<u>Meditative Impressions</u>

65

"The giving of love is an education in itself."
–Eleanor Roosevelt

<u>Meditative Impressions</u>

67

"Don't forget to love yourself."
–Soren Kierkegaard

<u>Meditative Impressions</u>

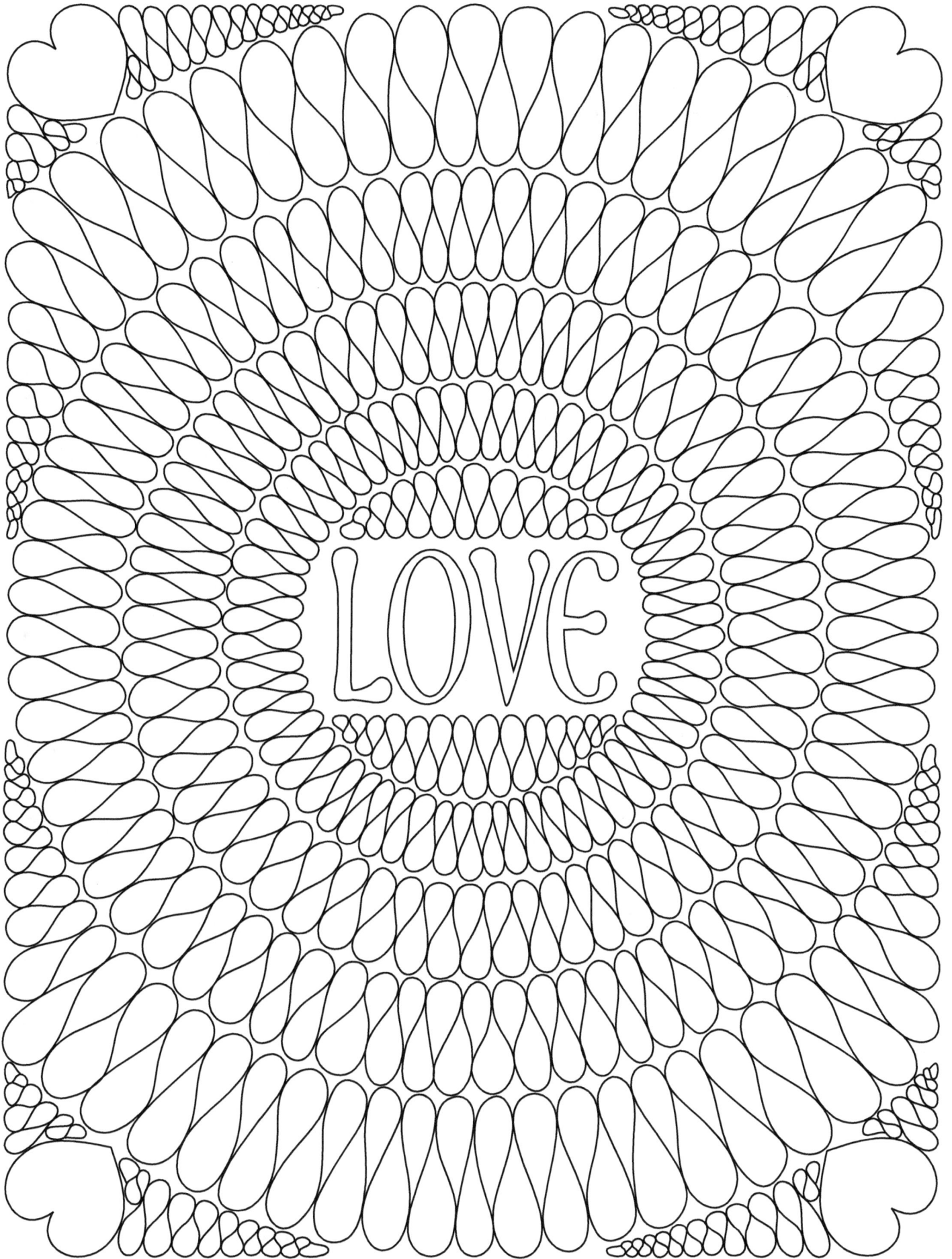

LOVE

69

"Not all of us can do great things, but we can do small things with great love."

–Mother Teresa

<u>Meditative Impressions</u>

71

"Love comforts like sunshine after rain."
         –William Shakespeare

<u>Meditative Impressions</u>

73

"Love is of all passions the strongest, for it attacks simultaneously the head, the heart, and the senses."

-Lao Tzu

Meditative Impressions

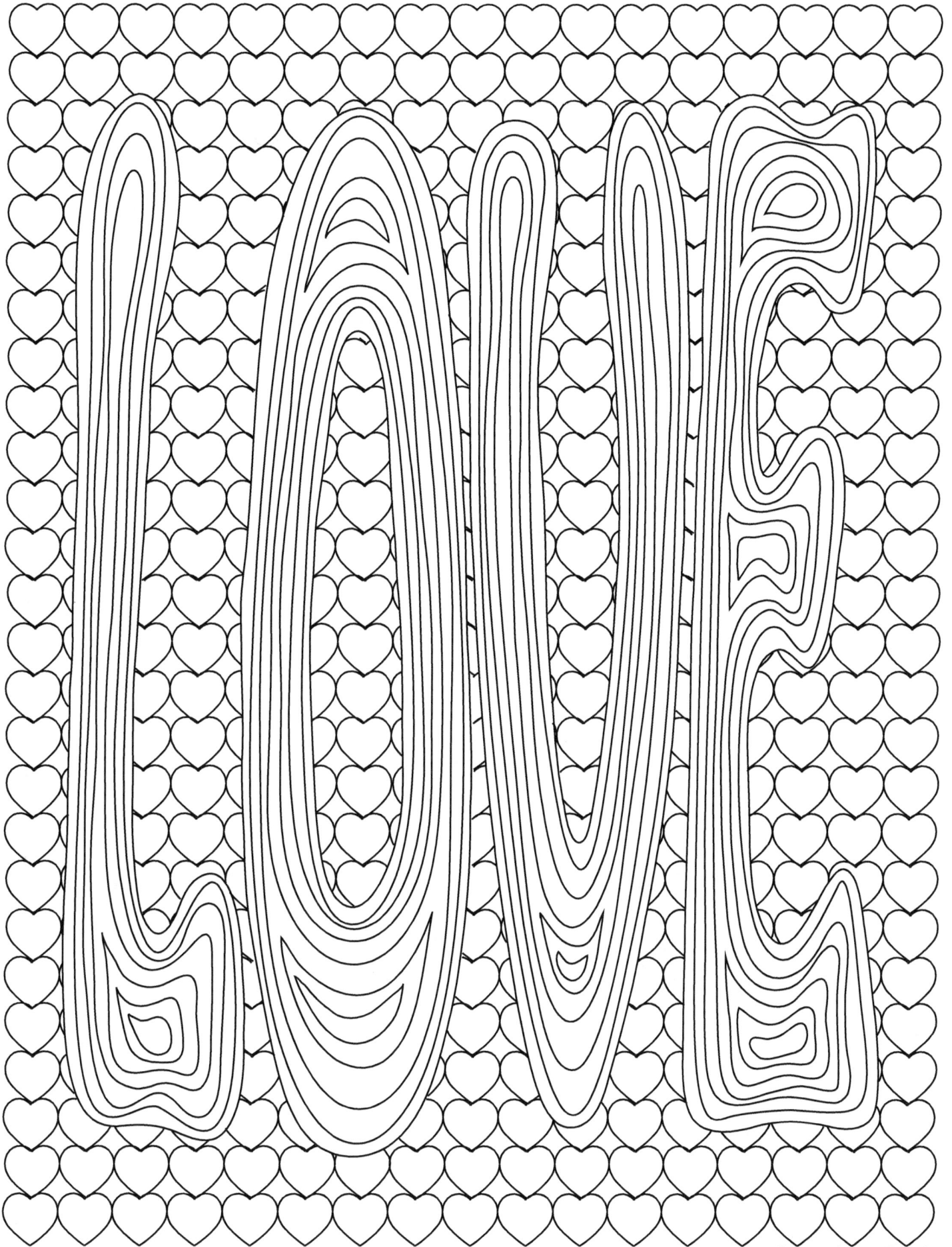

"Get on with living and loving. You don't have forever."
–Leo Buscaglia

<u>Meditative Impressions</u>

"If you would be loved, love, and be lovable."
-*Benjamin Franklin*

<u>Meditative Impressions</u>

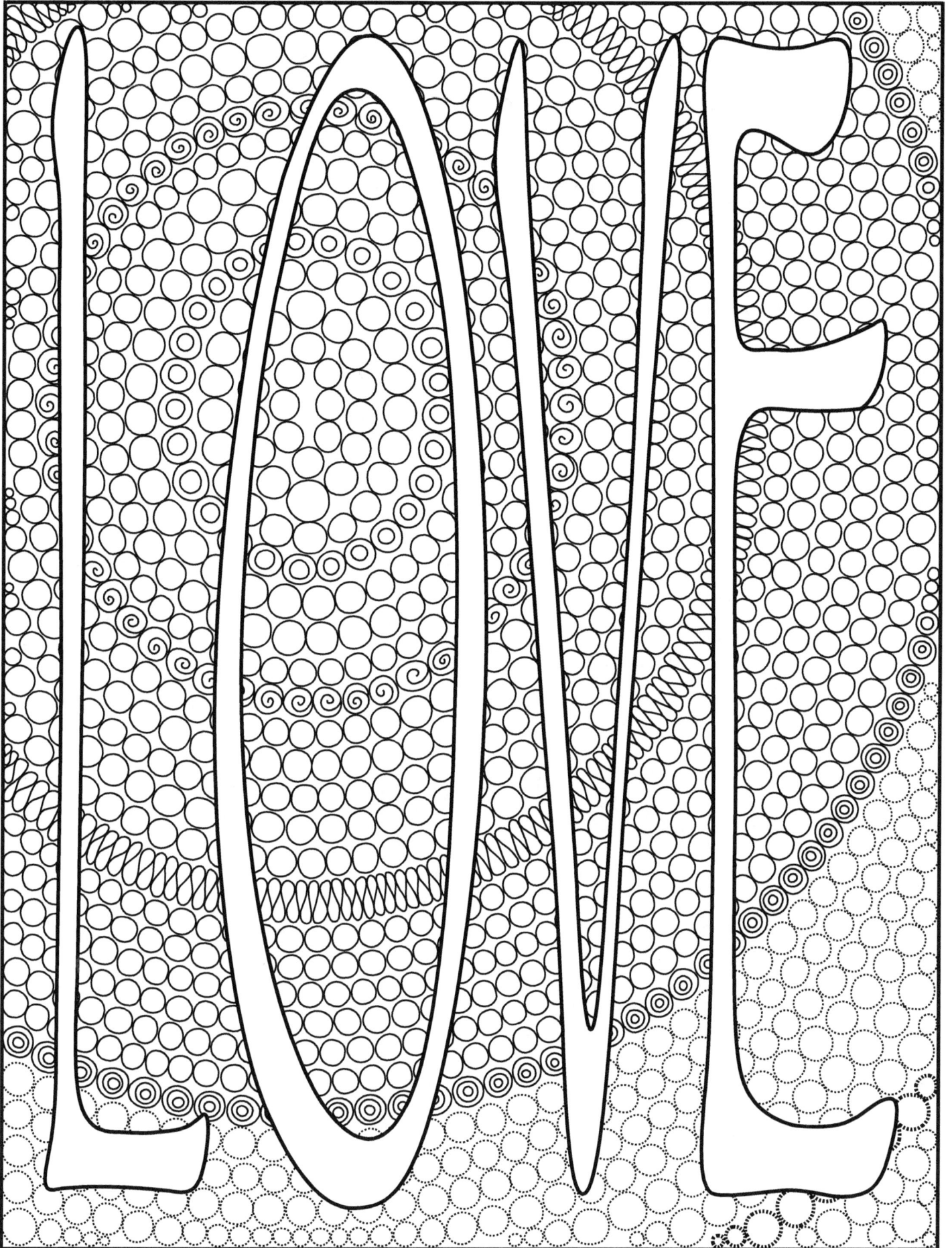

79

"At the touch of love everyone becomes a poet."
                                        –Plato

Meditative Impressions

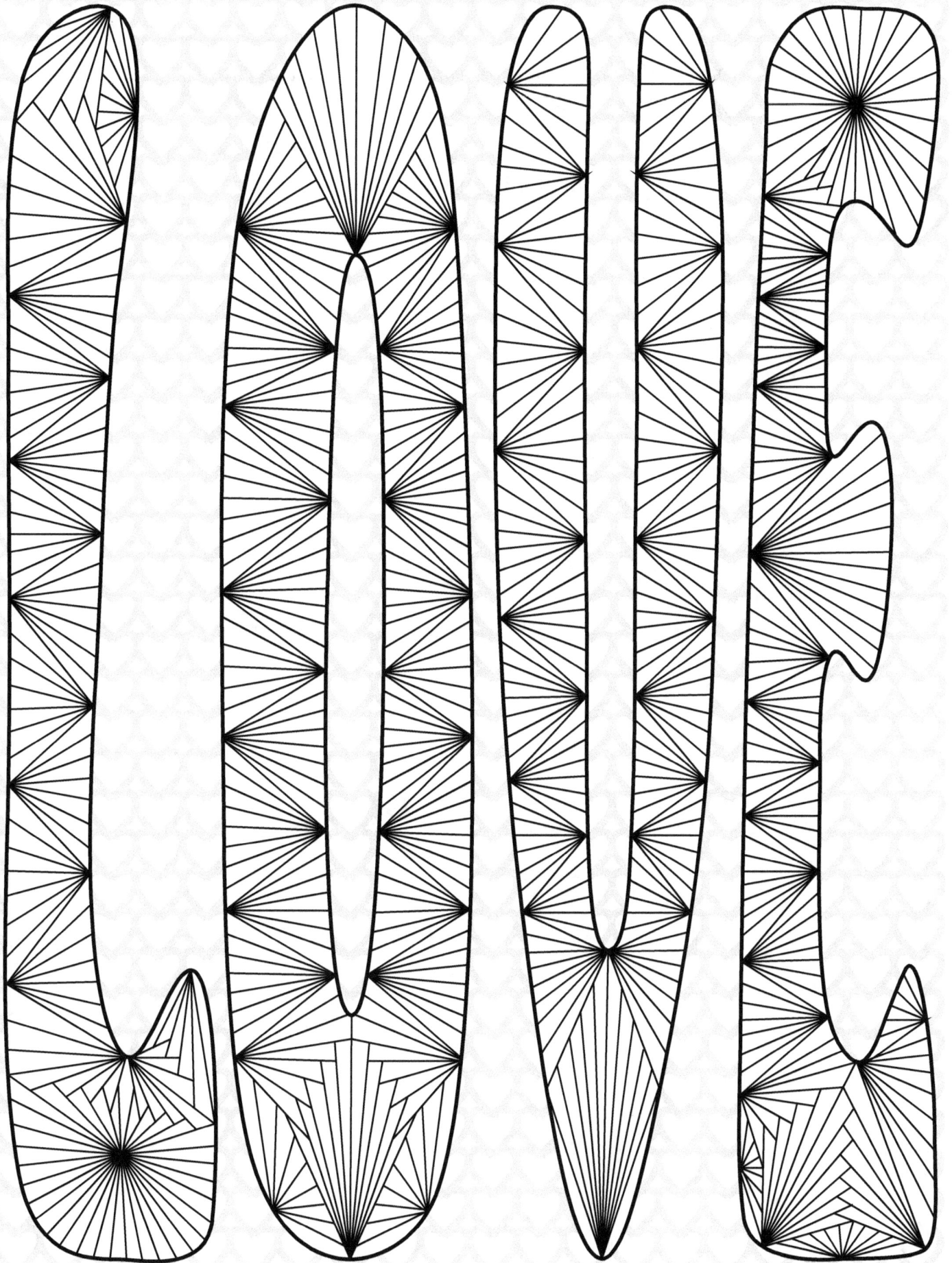

81

"You really have to love yourself to get anything done in this world."

–Lucille Ball

Meditative Impressions

83

"Gravitation is not respsonsible for people falling in love."
-Albert Einstein

<u>Meditative Impressions</u>

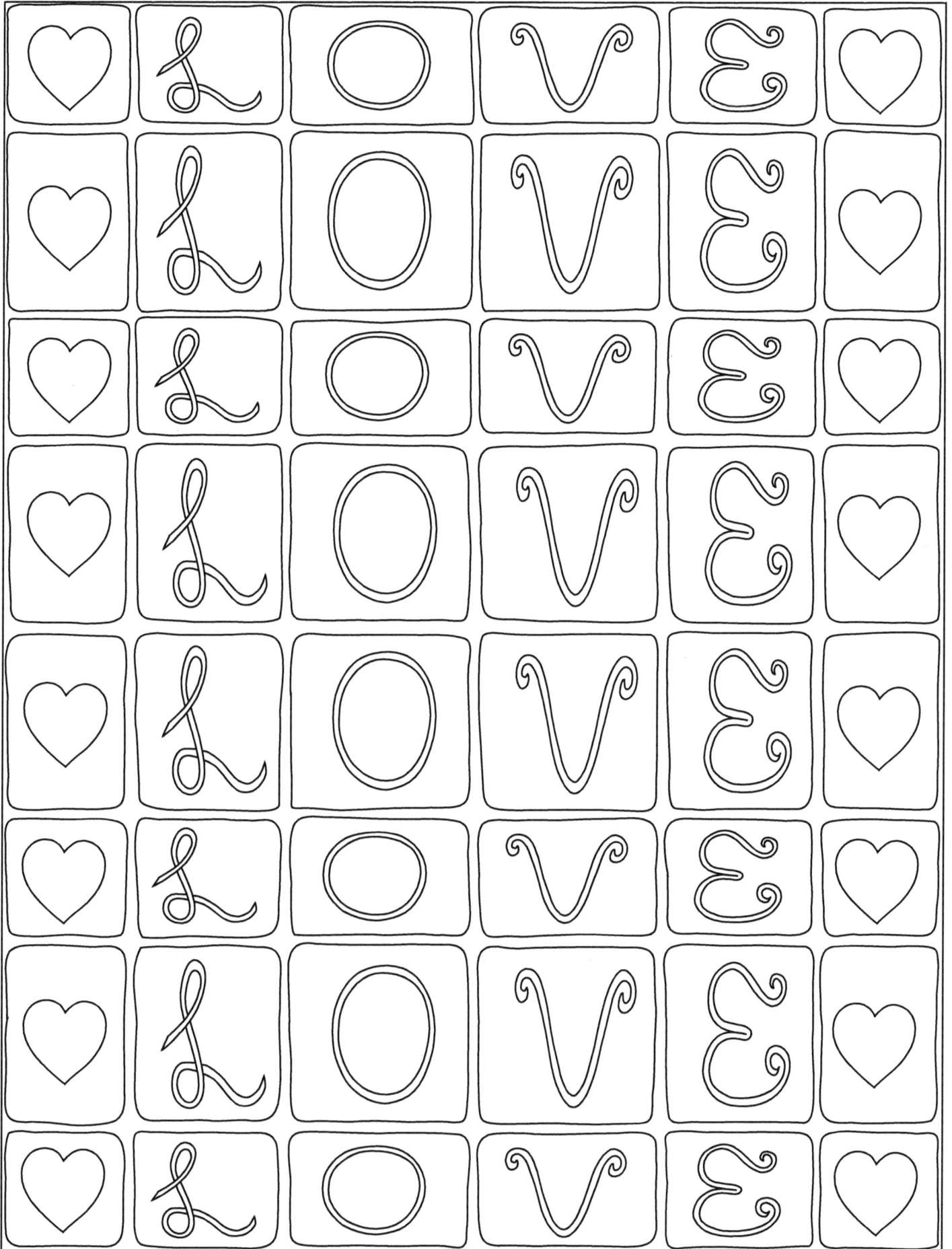

"Where there is love there is life."
–Mahatma Gandhi

Meditative Impressions

87

"Don't cry because it's over, smile because it happened."
                                           –Dr. Seuss

Meditative Impressions

89

"All you need is love. But a little chocolate now and then doesn't hurt."

–Charles Schulz

<u>Meditative Impressions</u>

© 2016 Aliyah Schick

Romantic Novels

Romeo and Juliet, William Shakespeare, 1597

Sense and Sensibility, Jane Austen, 1811

Pride and Prejudice, Jane Austen, 1813

Emma, Jane Austen, 1815

The Count of Monte Cristo, Alexandre Dumas, 1844

Jane Eyre, Charlotte Bronte, 1847

Wuthering Heights, Emily Bronte, 1847

Vanity Fair, William Makepeace Thackeray, 1847

The Scarlet Letter, Nathaniel Hawthorne, 1850

Madame Bovary, Gustave Flaubert, 1856

Little Women, Louisa May Alcott, 1868

Middlemarch, George Elliot, 1872

Anna Karenina, Leo Tolstoy, 1878

Tess of the D'Urbervilles, Thomas Hardy, 1891

The Awakening, Kate Chopin, 1899

A Room with a View, EM Forster, 1908

Anne of Green Gables, L.M. Montgomery, 1908

The Phantom of the Opera, Gaston Leroux, 1909

Death in Venice, Thomas Mann, 1912

Sons and Lovers, D.H. Lawrence, 1913

The Great Gatsby, F. Scott Fitzgerald, 1925

Gone with the Wind, Margaret Mitchell, 1936

Rebecca, Daphne du Maurier, 1938

Doctor Zhivago, Boris Pasternak, 1957

The Graduate, Charles Webb, 1963

The French Lieutenant's Woman, John Fowles, 1969

The Princess Bride, William Goldman, 1973

The Thorn Birds, Colleen McCullough, 1977

The Far Pavilions, M. M. Kaye, 1978

Love in the Time of Cholera, Gabriel Garcia Marquez, 1985

The Remains of the Day, Kazuo Ishiguro, 1989

The English Patient, Michael Ondaatje, 1992

The Notebook, Nicholas Sparks, 1996

Atonement, Ian McEwan, 2001

It Happened One Autumn, Lisa Kleypas, 2005

Romantic Comedy Movies

It Happened One Night, 1934, Clark Gable, Claudette Colbert
Bringing Up Baby, 1938, Cary Grant, Katherine Hepburn
The Shop Around the Corner, 1940, Jimmy Stewart, Margaret Sullivan
The African Queen, 1951, Katherine Hepburn, Humphrey Bogart
An Affair to Remember, 1957, Cary Grant, Deborah Kerr
The Graduate, 1967, Dustin Hoffman, Anne Bancroft
Harold and Maude, 1971, Bud Cort, Ruth Gordon
Annie Hall, 1977, Woody Allen, Diane Keaton
Splash, 1984, Tom Hanks, Daryl Hannah
Roxanne, 1987, Steve Martin, Daryl Hannah
Moonstruck, 1987, Cher, Nicholas Cage
When Harry Met Sally, 1989, Billy Crystal, Meg Ryan
Pretty Woman, 1990, Richard Gere, Julia Roberts
Sleepless in Seattle, 1993, Tom Hanks, Meg Ryan
Groundhog Day, 1993, Bill Murray, Andie MacDowell
Four Weddings and a Funeral, 1994, Hugh Grant, Andie MacDowell
My Best Friend's Wedding, 1997, Julia Roberts, Dermot Mulroney
Shakespeare in Love, 1998, Gwyneth Paltrow, Joseph Fiennes
You've Got Mail, 1998, Tom Hanks, Meg Ryan
Notting Hill, 1999, Hugh Grant, Julia Roberts

© 2016 Aliyah Schick

© 2016 Aliyah Schick

Runaway Bride, 1999, Julia Roberts, Richard Gere
Meet the Parents, 2000, Ben Stiller, Robert De Niro
The Wedding Planner, 2001, Jennifer Lopez, Matthew McConaughey
Bridget Jones's Diary, 2001, Renee Zellweger, Colin Firth, Hugh Grant
Sweet Home Alabama, 2002, Reese Witherspoon, Patrick Dempsey
How to Lose a Guy in 10 Days, 2003, Kate Hudson, Matthew McConaughey
Something's Gotta Give, 2003, Jack Nicholson, Diane Keaton
Spanglish, 2004, Adam Sandler, Tea Leoni, Paz Vega
50 First Dates, 2004, Adam Sandler, Drew Barrymore
Must Love Dogs, 2005, Diane Lane, John Cusack
The Wedding Date, 2005, Dermot Mulroney, Debra Messing
Imagine Me & You, 2005, Piper Perabo, Lena Headey
Failure to Launch, 2006, Matthew McConaughey, Sarah Jessica Parker
No Reservations, 2007, Catherine Zeta-Jones, Aaron Eckhart, Abigail Breslin
Mamma Mia!, 2008, Meryl Streep, Pierce Brosnan
27 Dresses, 2008, Katherine Heigl, James Marsden
Sex and the City, 2008, Sarah Jessica Parker
The Proposal, 2009, Sandra Bullock, Ryan Reynolds
Friends with Benefits, 2011, Mila Kunis, Justin Timberlake

Love Songs of the 50's

- "Mona Lisa," Nat King Cole, 1950
- "You Belong to Me," Jo Stafford, 1952
- "Your Cheatin' Heart," Hank Williams Sr., 1952
- "That's Amore," Dean Martin, 1953
- "Earth Angel," The Penguins, 1954
- "In the Still of the Nite," The Five Satins, 1956
- "Why Do Fools Fall in Love," Frankie Lymon & The Teenagers, 1956
- "Bye Bye Love," Everly Brothers, 1957
- "Lonely Teardrops," Jackie Wilson, 1958
- "You're So Fine," The Falcons, 1959

Love Songs of the 60's

- "Stand By Me," Ben E. King, 1961
- "At Last," Etta James, 1961
- "Can't Help Falling in Love with You," Elvis Presley, 1961
- "My Girl," The Temptations, 1964
- "In My Life," The Beatles, 1965
- "I Can't Help Myself," The Four Tops, 1965
- "Unchained Melody," Righteous Brothers, 1965
- "God Only Knows," The Beach Boys, 1966
- "River Deep, Mountain High," Tina Turner, 1966
- "When a Man Loves a Woman," Percy Sledge, 1966
- "(You Make Me Feel Like) A Natural Woman," Aretha Franklin, 1967
- "The Look of Love," Dusty Springfield, 1967
- "Ain't No Mountain High Enough," Marvin Gaye and Tammi Terrell, 1967
- "Sweet Thing," Van Morrison, 1968
- "Lay Lady Lay," Bob Dylan, 1969

Love Songs of the 70's

- "Your Song," Elton John, 1970
- "Let's Stay Together," Al Green, 1971
- "The First Time Ever I Saw Your Face," Roberta Flack, 1972
- "You are the Sunshine of My Life," Stevie Wonder, 1973
- "Then Came You," Dionne Warwick and The Spinners, 1974
- "Can't Get Enough of Your Love," Babe, Barry White, 1974
- "Baby I Love Your Way," Peter Frampton, 1975
- "Love to Love Baby," Donna Summer, 1975
- "Nobody Does It Better," Carly Simon, 1977

Love Songs of the 80's

- "Endless Love," Diana Ross and Lionel Richie, 1981
- "Precious," The Jam, 1982
- "Up Where We Belong," Jennifer Warnes and Joe Cocker, 1982
- "This Must Be the Place," Talking Heads, 1983
- "Time After Time," Cyndi Lauper, 1983
- "Ain't Nobody," Chaka Khan and Rufus, 1983
- "Hello," Lionel Richie, 1984
- "I Just Called to Say I Love You," Stevie Wonder, 1984
- "What's Love Got to Do with It," Tina Turner, 1984
- "Against All Odds (Take a Look at Me Now)," Phil Collins, 1984
- "Careless Whisper," George Michael, 1984
- "Joanna," Kool and the Gang, 1984
- "Saving All My Love for You," Whitney Houston, 1985
- "Sweet Love," Anita Baker, 1986
- "So Amazing," Luther Vandross, 1987
- "The Way You Make Me Feel," Michael Jackson, 1987
- "Adore," Prince, 1987

Love Songs of the 90's

- "Emotions," Mariah Carey, 1991
- "(Everything I Do) I Do It for You," Bryan Adams, 1991
- "I Will Always Love You," Whitney Houston, 1992
- "I'll Make Love to You," Boyz II Men, 1994
- "Can You Feel the Love Tonight," Elton John, 1994
- "I'll Stand by You," The Pretenders, 1994
- "Kiss from a Rose," Seal, 1994
- "You Were Meant for Me," Jewel, 1995
- "Higher," D'Angelo, 1995
- "One in a Million," Aaliyah, 1996
- "Everlong," Foo Fighters, 1997
- "As Long as You Love Me," Backstreet Boys, 1997
- "All My Life," K-Ci and JoJo, 1998
- "I Don't Wanna Miss a Thing," Aerosmith, 1998
- "You're Still the One," Shania Twain, 1998
- "I Wanna Grow Old with You," Adam Sandler, 1998
- "You Got Me," The Roots, 1999

Love Songs of the 2000's

- "I Hope You Dance," Lee Ann Womack, 2000
- "Yellow," Coldplay, 2000
- "Underneath It All," No Doubt (Gwen Stefani), 2001
- "Fallin'," Alicia Keys, 2002
- "Come Away with Me," Norah Jones, 2002
- "Bonnie and Clyde," Jay-Z, 2002
- "Somebody Like You," Keith Urban, 2002
- "You'll Think of Me," Keith Urban, 2002
- "A Moment Like This," Kelly Clarkson, 2002
- "If I Ain't Got You," Alicia Keys, 2003
- "Crazy in Love," Beyonce, 2003
- "Remember When," Alan Jackson, 2003
- "Throwback," Usher, 2004
- "Live Like You Were Dying," Tim McGraw, 2004
- "We Belong Together," Mariah Carey, 2005
- "My Love," Justin Timberlake, 2006
- "Chasing Cars," Snow Patrol, 2006
- "Falling Slowly," The Swell Season, 2007
- "You Belong with Me," Taylor Swift, 2008
- "Make You Feel My Love," Adele, 2008
- "Love Story," Taylor Swift, 2008
- "In These Arms," The Swell Season, 2009
- "You Raise Me Up," Josh Groban, 2009
- "Need You Now," Lady Antebellum, 2009
- "I Gotta Feeling," The Black Eyed Peas, 2009

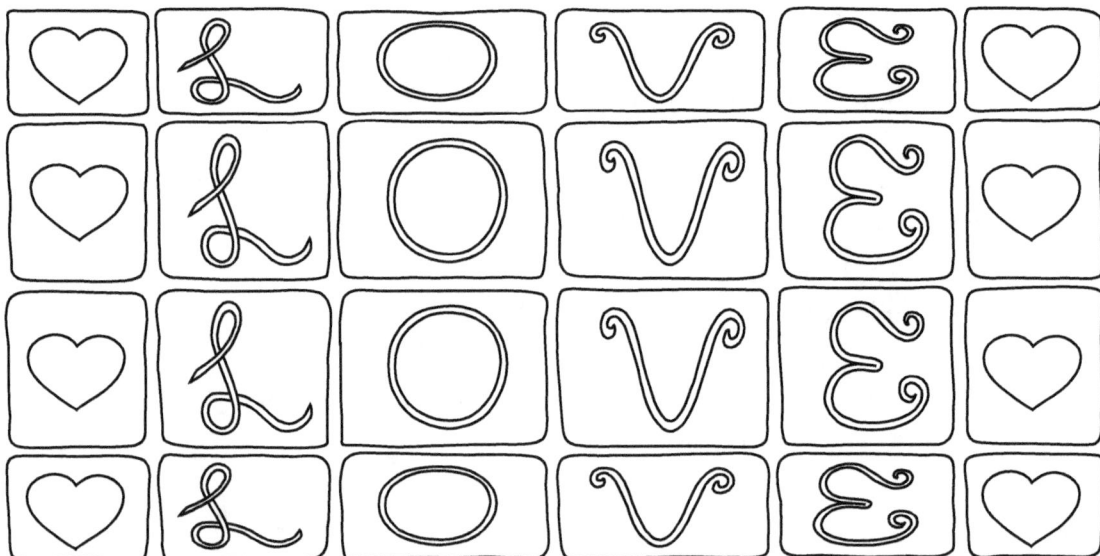

More Meditative Coloring Books

by
Aliyah Schick

The Meditative Coloring Books Series:
Angels, Crosses, Ancient Symbols, Hearts, Labyrinths, OM, and Goddess

Meditative Coloring Book 1 -- Angels

These angelic images are drawn with a pen in each hand, as artist Aliyah Schick allows the lines to go where they will, mirroring each other. Every movement is guided by spirit; every drawing is different; and each one is a wonderful surprise filled with angelic presence. Immerse yourself in the angelic realm as you color these drawings. Invite the angels to come into your world, to love and support you in all you do.

Meditative Coloring Book 2 -- Crosses

The cross is one of the most ancient and enduring sacred symbols, found in nearly every culture from cave dwellers throughout human existence. It symbolizes the celestial, spiritual divine coming into being in this material world. It represents the sacred taking form, and the integration of soul into physical life. These 36 original artist's drawings feature ancient and contemporary images of the cross in reflections of the deep spiritual significance of its form. Let the spirit and meaning of the cross fill you as you color these images.

Meditative Coloring Book 3 -- Ancient Symbols

Ancient and indigenous sacred images speak deeply to us, to our bellies and our bones, to our cellular memory and our wisdom, to our souls' yearnings. Native peoples throughout time and place see the sacred in all of life. For them, holiness is life and life is holiness. Life is the manifestation of the holy in all things. These original artist's drawings feature timeless designs used by every culture on earth to remind us of the sacred. Dip into deeply meaningful realms as you color these drawings.

Meditative Coloring Book 4 -- Hearts

The heart is one of our favorite symbols, evoking feelings of love, caring, loyalty, and devotion. As you spend time with these heart drawings, open your heart to live with more compassion for others and for yourself. Open your life to deeper connection with the earth and all of life. Open yourself to recognize the sacred in all things, including in yourself.

www.MeditativeColoring.com

Meditative Coloring Book 5 -- Labyrinths

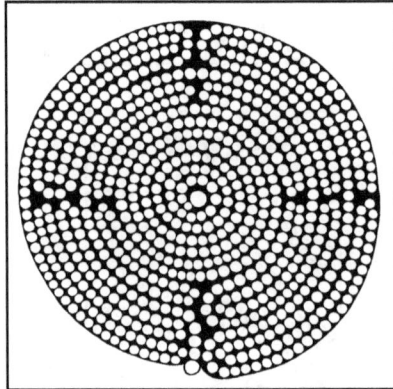

Color your steps into the labyrinth as you contemplate, meditate, or pray. Go deep into your inner wisdom and guidance where questions' answers reveal themselves and choices come clear. Or, simply relax and be with your breathing. Now you can bring your labyrinth with you to wherever you need to be. This collection of 36 original artist's drawings invites you into the labyrinth any time you wish.

Meditative Coloring Book 6 -- OM

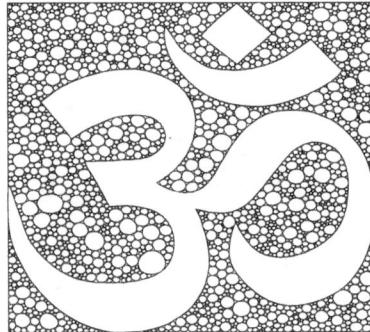

Spend meditative time with the *OM* as you color these 36 original artist's drawings. Allow the *OM* to infuse and entune your spirit, your mind, your emotions, and every cell of your body with its pure, sacred grace. Fill yourself with its light. Become one with its beauty. Emerge relaxed, centered, calm, and at peace.

Color for relaxation, stress reduction, meditation, spiritual connection, prayer, centering, and healing. Color to calm and come into balance, to find your intuitive wisdom, and to learn to be more of your deep, true self.

Meditative Coloring Book 7 -- Goddess

For 30,000 years in prehistoric time people all over the world celebrated and worshipped the sacred feminine. The Great Mother Goddess was the creator of all life and the life force within all life. Worship was every day here and now, holistic, visceral and sensual, all about earth, body, and nature.

Now we are seeing a revival of the sacred feminine through valuing nature, simplicity, mindfulness, meaningfulness, and clarity, along with a growing desire to honor intuition, right-brain knowing, and deep connection.

Color these 36 original artist's drawings as you open yourself to the sacred feminine in you. Nurture this long-abandoned side of conscious living, and bring yourself to a more sustainable balance.

The Labyrinth Guided Journal, a Year in the Labyrinth

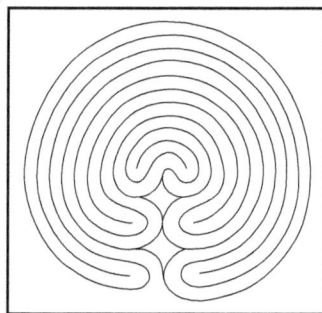

The twists and turns of the labyrinth remove you from ordinary life, and draw you deeper into willingness, into yourself, and into sacred wisdom. Use *The Labyrinth Guided Journal* on your own journey through the next year. Each week the journal offers a new thought or experience or challenge drawn from the labyrinth, and a question or suggestion for you to consider and write about throughout the week.

The Jewish Coloring Books for Grown Ups

Color for stress relaxation, Jewish meditation, Shabbat peace, and healing.

JUDAICA Coloring Book

Menorah, dredel, Ten Commandment tablets, challah, Torah scrolls, Magen David, Havdalah braid, mezuzah, and more. Color these beautiful, original artist's drawings based on familiar Jewish objects and symbols. Relax, unwind, de-stress, and allow healing as you ground yourself into your Jewish heritage. L'chaim!

ALEFBET Coloring Book

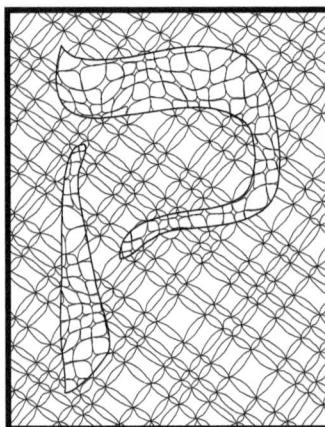

Alef, bet, gimel, dalet, hey, vav, zayin, chet, tet, yod, kaf, lamed, mem, nun, samech, ayin, peh, tsade, qof, resh, shin, and tav; 22 letters in the Hebrew alefbet. Coloring these 36 beautiful, original artist's drawings based on the Hebrew letter forms is relaxing, reduces stress, and lightens your load as it connects you with your Jewish roots. If these letters are the building blocks of the universe, then spending peaceful time coloring them can be beneficial in deeply healing ways, too.

CHAI Coloring Book

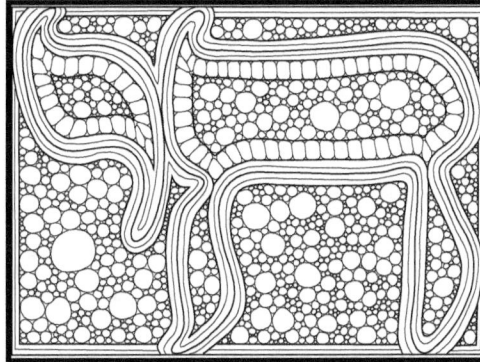

The Jewish *Chai* symbol represents the Hebrew word *chai*, meaning life. It is worn, displayed, or given as a gift as a symbol and reminder of the Jewish love for life, to celebrate being Jewish, and to bring abundant good luck. Spend relaxed, meditative time immersed in the many joys of the *Chai* as you color these 36 beautiful drawings.

STAR OF DAVID Coloring Book

The six-pointed Star of David is our most familiar Jewish symbol. Used as decoration and adornment on both religious and secular items, the Star of David represents Jewish pride in shared heritage, community, and family, and a declaration of hope and commitment. Spend time coloring these 36 original artist's drawings based on the Star of David and allow yourself to ground into your Jewish roots and celebrate your love of being Jewish.

Sacred Imprints

www.ingramcontent.com/pod-product-compliance
Lightning Source LLC
LaVergne TN
LVHW081318060426
835509LV00015B/1572